Learning with the Animals

The Alphabet
Letters & Words

Fairytale and Illustrations
Carmen Zeta

WINSOR
PUBLISHING

Winsor Publishing

All rights reserved; no part of this publication may be reproduced or transmitted by any means, electronic, mechanical, photocopying or otherwise, without the prior written permission of the publisher except for the use of brief quotations in a book review.

First published in Great Britain in 2024
by Winsor Publishing

1st Edition

Copyright © Winsor Publishing 2024
Copyright of Text (fairytale) © Carmen Zeta (Tsoutsoumanou) 2024
Copyright of Text (exercises) © Constantin Rosso Corvin

ISBN: 978-1-913881-15-3

www.WinsorPublishing.com

About the Author

Carmen Zeta was born in Iași, Romania, a beautiful and historic city, known for the start of the Greek Revolution of 1821.

She received her medical degree from the University of Gr. T. Popa in 1987. After obtaining her cardiology specialty in Athens, she moved to Heraklion, Crete in 2000. She worked for almost 20 years at the Venizelio General Hospital of Heraklion as a cardiologist.

Her relationship with painting began in her teenage years. She started as a self-taught artist, and has attended many educational seminars, while she has also participated in a painting exhibition of the Medical Association of Heraklion in 2017 at the Basilica of Saint Mark.
She has also taken painting lessons with the internationally renowned artist Botis Thalassinos.

In 2019, she became the grandmother of a girl named Carmen, who stole her heart for the second time in her life, as she had felt again with the birth of her only son Dimitris.

The series of books "Learning with the Animals" is dedicated to little Carmen, as the motivation to have beautiful educational books to learn to write and read. It was also the starting point for the creation of the series.

Introduction

The idea of this book began when I realized that the time is now approaching for my beloved granddaughter's long journey into the world of letters, knowledge, imagination, and creation.
Her Will to learn, the strength of her soul reflected in her big, beautiful eyes full of questions, was my inspiration. She guided me step by step in the creation of this book.
It is the least I could do, to support her wonderful endeavor with all my might. To sweeten as much as possible the difficulties of a beginning, for her but also for all the children of the same age, and not only, who share the same anxieties, but also the great joy of every new beginning. This little tale and the drawings, I hope, will awaken the desire to conquer the secrets of a hidden treasure that will remain imprinted in the children's memory as the first wonderful experience of an educational book where the letters will come to life and become part of a hidden code that only those who know how to decode it, will be able to solve countless secrets and it will open horizons for them to conquer their dreams... the magic code of language!
Although I am neither a professional illustrator nor a writer, it is the love of a grandmother who adores her grandchild that prompted me to create this book. Nothing more simple and honest, like the love of many millions of grandmothers around the world who experience the same feelings as me.

To our little star,
and to all those who love truthfully.

Carmen Zeta

Once Upon a Time

there was a large family of many different animals, which lived in many parts of the world. Some in the same country, some in different countries and continents, some in lakes, rivers, seas, oceans, forests, the desert, on farms. They were all kinds of animals, mammals, birds, insects, from the smallest and fragile to gigantic in height and weight. They lived in love, in harmony with nature, but they had one complaint...

They could not meet and above all communicate with each other, share their news, how they spend their time, what games they play, because of the great distance that separated them.

Days passed and their sadness grew. Until one day all the animals in the forest of a tropical island decided to gather and hold a meeting to find a solution.

Having managed against all odds to meet, the convention began...

The sly fox suggested they shout loudly, the parrot to talk and sing, the dolphin to whistle, the birds to chirp...

Each tried to communicate with the other with the sound and language they knew by shouting as loud as they could to be heard. But no one knew how to write, no one had gone to school to learn letters, and this made their effort difficult.

After much thought the wise owl called out:
"I found it! I found it! I know how we will communicate with our relatives and friends from all over the world. We will make a communication code consisting of several letters. Each animal will contribute the first letter of its name to the creation of this code and we will call it the "alphabet". With all the letters we will be able to write words, then complete sentences. Thus, we will describe our daily lives, how we spend time at school, on vacation with our family or with our friends".

Everyone happily agreed and the pigeon took it upon himself to be the postman who would send all these letters and cards to their relatives and friends from all over the world.

So, let's start our journey with the first capital letter "A" given to us by our good friend the Angelfish and with the small "a" given to us by her baby.

A a A a

Angelfish

Write the following letter by tracing the lines:

a a a a a a a a a a a a a a

Write the letter without the help of the lines:

Try to write the entire name of the animal by tracing the lines:

Angelfish   Angelfish

Angelfish   Angelfish

Can you write the name of the animal without tracing the lines?

B b   B b

Butterfly

Write the following letter by tracing the lines:

b b b b b b b b b b b b

Write the letter without the help of the lines:

Try to write the entire name of the animal by tracing the lines:

Butterfly   Butterfly

Butterfly   Butterfly

Can you write the name of the animal without tracing the lines?

C c   C c

Cow

Write the following letter by tracing the lines:

C C C C C C C C C C C C C

Write the letter without the help of the lines:

Try to write the entire name of the animal by tracing the lines:

Cow Cow Cow Cow Cow
Cow Cow Cow Cow Cow

Can you write the name of the animal without tracing the lines?

D d   D d

Dog

Write the following letter by tracing the lines:

d d d d d d d d d d d d

Write the letter without the help of the lines:

Try to write the entire name of the animal by tracing the lines:

Dog Dog Dog Dog Dog

Dog Dog Dog Dog Dog

Can you write the name of the animal without tracing the lines?

E e   E e

Elephant

Write the following letter by tracing the lines:

e e e e e e e e e e e e e e

Write the letter without the help of the lines:

Try to write the entire name of the animal by tracing the lines:

Elephant   Elephant

Elephant   Elephant

Can you write the name of the animal without tracing the lines?

F f F f

Flamingo

Write the following letter by tracing the lines:

f f f f f f f f f f f f f f f f f f f

Write the letter without the help of the lines:

Try to write the entire name of the animal by tracing the lines:

Flamingo   Flamingo

Flamingo   Flamingo

Can you write the name of the animal without tracing the lines?

G g   G g

Giraffe

Write the following letter by tracing the lines:

g g g g g g g g g g g g g

Write the letter without the help of the lines:

Try to write the entire name of the animal by tracing the lines:

Giraffe   Giraffe   Giraffe

Giraffe   Giraffe   Giraffe

Can you write the name of the animal without tracing the lines?

H h   H h

Hippocampus

Write the following letter by tracing the lines:

h h h h h h h h h h h h

Write the letter without the help of the lines:

Try to write the entire name of the animal by tracing the lines:

Hippocampus

Hippocampus

Can you write the name of the animal without tracing the lines?

I i   I i

Ibis

Write the following letter by tracing the lines:

| | | | | | | | | | | | | | |

Write the letter without the help of the lines:

Try to write the entire name of the animal by tracing the lines:

Ibis   Ibis   Ibis   Ibis   Ibis
Ibis   Ibis   Ibis   Ibis   Ibis

Can you write the name of the animal without tracing the lines?

J j   J j

Jellyfish

Write the following letter by tracing the lines:

j j j j j j j j j j j j j j j j

Write the letter without the help of the lines:

Try to write the entire name of the animal by tracing the lines:

Jellyfish Jellyfish Jellyfish
Jellyfish Jellyfish Jellyfish

Can you write the name of the animal without tracing the lines?

K k K k

Kangaroo

Write the following letter by tracing the lines:

k k k k k k k k k k k k

Write the letter without the help of the lines:

Try to write the entire name of the animal by tracing the lines:

Kangaroo   Kangaroo

Kangaroo   Kangaroo

Can you write the name of the animal without tracing the lines?

L1 L1

Lion

Write the following letter by tracing the lines:

Write the letter without the help of the lines:

Try to write the entire name of the animal by tracing the lines:

Lion Lion Lion Lion
Lion Lion Lion Lion

Can you write the name of the animal without tracing the lines?

M m M m

Monkey

Write the following letter by tracing the lines:

m m m m m m m m m m

Write the letter without the help of the lines:

Try to write the entire name of the animal by tracing the lines:

Monkey Monkey Monkey
Monkey Monkey Monkey

Can you write the name of the animal without tracing the lines?

N n   N n

Numbat

Write the following letter by tracing the lines:

n n n n n n n n n n n n

Write the letter without the help of the lines:

Try to write the entire name of the animal by tracing the lines:

Numbat Numbat Numbat
Numbat Numbat Numbat

Can you write the name of the animal without tracing the lines?

O o O o

Octopus

Write the following letter by tracing the lines:

o o o o o o o o o o o o o o

Write the letter without the help of the lines:

Try to write the entire name of the animal by tracing the lines:

Octopus   Octopus

Octopus   Octopus

Can you write the name of the animal without tracing the lines?

P p   P p

Penguin

Write the following letter by tracing the lines:

p p p p p p p p p p p p

Write the letter without the help of the lines:

Try to write the entire name of the animal by tracing the lines:

Penguin Penguin Penguin

Penguin Penguin Penguin

Can you write the name of the animal without tracing the lines?

Q q   Q q

Quetzal

Write the following letter by tracing the lines:

q q q q q q q q q q

Write the letter without the help of the lines:

Try to write the entire name of the animal by tracing the lines:

Quetzal Quetzal Quetzal
Quetzal Quetzal Quetzal

Can you write the name of the animal without tracing the lines?

R r　　　　　　　　　　　　　R r

Rhinoceros

Write the following letter by tracing the lines:

r r r r r r r r r r r r r r r r r r r r r r r r r

Write the letter without the help of the lines:

Try to write the entire name of the animal by tracing the lines:

Rhinoceros   Rhinoceros

Rhinoceros   Rhinoceros

Can you write the name of the animal without tracing the lines?

S s   S s

Swordfish

Write the following letter by tracing the lines:

S S S S S S S S S S S

Write the letter without the help of the lines:

Try to write the entire name of the animal by tracing the lines:

Swordfish   Swordfish

Swordfish   Swordfish

Can you write the name of the animal without tracing the lines?

T t   T t

Tiger

Write the following letter by tracing the lines:

t t t t t t t t t t t t t t t t t

Write the letter without the help of the lines:

Try to write the entire name of the animal by tracing the lines:

Tiger Tiger Tiger Tiger
Tiger Tiger Tiger Tiger

Can you write the name of the animal without tracing the lines?

U u   U u

Unau

Write the following letter by tracing the lines:

U U U U U U U U U U U U U U U

Write the letter without the help of the lines:

Try to write the entire name of the animal by tracing the lines:

Unau   Unau   Unau   Unau

Unau   Unau   Unau   Unau

Can you write the name of the animal without tracing the lines?

V v   V v

Vicuna

Write the following letter by tracing the lines:

V V V V V V V V V V V V V

Write the letter without the help of the lines:

Try to write the entire name of the animal by tracing the lines:

Vicuna   Vicuna   Vicuna

Vicuna   Vicuna   Vicuna

Can you write the name of the animal without tracing the lines?

W w   W w

Weasel

Write the following letter by tracing the lines:

W W W W W W W W W W

Write the letter without the help of the lines:

Try to write the entire name of the animal by tracing the lines:

Weasel Weasel Weasel
Weasel Weasel Weasel

Can you write the name of the animal without tracing the lines?

X x   X x

Xerus

Write the following letter by tracing the lines:

X X X X X X X X X X X X X X X

Write the letter without the help of the lines:

Try to write the entire name of the animal by tracing the lines:

Xerus Xerus Xerus Xerus

Xerus Xerus Xerus Xerus

Can you write the name of the animal without tracing the lines?

Y y Y y

Yak

Write the following letter by tracing the lines:

y y y y y y y y y y y y y

Write the letter without the help of the lines:

Try to write the entire name of the animal by tracing the lines:

Yak Yak Yak Yak Yak

Yak Yak Yak Yak Yak

Can you write the name of the animal without tracing the lines?

Z z Z z

Zebra

Write the following letter by tracing the lines:

z z z z z z z z z z z z z z

Write the letter without the help of the lines:

Try to write the entire name of the animal by tracing the lines:

Zebra   Zebra   Zebra

Zebra   Zebra   Zebra

Can you write the name of the animal without tracing the lines?

www.ingramcontent.com/pod-product-compliance
Lightning Source LLC
Chambersburg PA
CBHW042020090526
44590CB00029B/4342